Army Flight School

Everything You Need to Know Before and During Flight School

Prep-Guide & Buyer's Guide

Table of Contents

Introduction

My name is Dexter Xavier, an Army officer in the Reserve component. When I was halfway through college, having no idea what would happen upon graduation, I decided to join ROTC and do something with my life. I worked very hard throughout the remainder of my college years to maintain a good GPA. I put all my efforts toward my ROTC training, and as a result, I was incredibly fortunate to attain one of the very few flight school slots at Fort Rucker, Alabama, home of Army Aviation.

Whether you're currently a soldier, a high school kid who always wanted to fly, or just curious about how the military guys do it, this guide will definitely help you. It contains the information that Fort Rucker students usually learn the hard way, the things flight school students pick up along the way, and the things we all wish we had known ahead of time.

However, because a fair amount of the information Army Flight School deals with is classified, this guide will not divulge any confidential information that would require you to have a clearance in order to access. What this guide will do is direct you to the best sources of information and impart to you the knowledge that will remove the stress related to becoming an Army pilot.

Getting a Slot

Army pilots are the ones who soar into the air beating it into submission as we come soaring overhead, bringing raining steel, medical evacuation, or any number of critical air support missions the units deem necessary. Slots for Army flight school are highly coveted by many soldiers and future soldiers alike. For obvious reasons, these slots are very expensive, and the competition for them very intense. Soldiers with shiny service records and lots of good reviews receive waivers to get there, despite the Army's bleeding budget and mile long litigations. Soldiers with no experience must jump through countless hurdles, usually, before being accepted.

If you are truly serious about working toward achieving your dream of becoming an Army Aviator, your first step is to find out whether you qualify. You can do a quick search on the internet and figure out all the necessary qualifications to be accepted into flight school. In *Appendix B* you will find some sites that will be very useful during your research. The Army Publishing Directorate will give any person with access to the internet information on the necessary paperwork required. There are a couple of Publications links in *Appendix B* that can help you find the documents necessary. Certain files on both of these pages will only give you access if you have CAC access. A CAC, or Common Access Card, is the identification card issued to you when you join the military.

If you're currently serving in the military, you should go to your leadership and tell them you want to file a packet for flight school. There is some good information on the USAREC (United States Army Recruiting Command) website if you look for Warrant Officer Recruiting. Many would agree that WOC School isn't a fun experience. However, warrant officers make excellent pilots, and typically don't end up in the same leadership roles as lieutenants and captains. Commissioned officers are hired as leaders. The Army needs leadership in every job we have. Lieutenants are pilots as well as leaders, and usually fly less than warrant officers after their initial assignments. Warrant officers usually handle different responsibility, such as unit safety officer. This means that they are responsible for a lot of work, but do not directly affect the lives of soldiers serving under them to the same degree as their platoon leader, who is a commissioned officer. Eight weeks of WOC School is a repeat of basic training, but it will be a quicker alternative to three months of OCS, or four years of ROTC. These slots are not easy to come by, and you will need to pass a board to be selected.

Most jaded Army guys will tell you that it's all about who you know. In my limited experience, in some instances they are correct. A friend from AIT (Advanced Individual Training) happened to know someone on his selection board, and consequently his entire interview lasted about fifteen minutes. That isn't to say he wasn't qualified; the guy will be an amazing pilot. However, the guy who went through before him, although he had better scores, his board interview lasted more than an hour, and after it concluded he left sweating and unsettled.

For those soldiers who don't know someone on a flight board, find a leader in your unit who would be willing to write you a good recommendation. Choose a stellar performer, whose record will carry some weight. Don't just ask a buddy or an officer simply because they like you or you like them. Ask the officer or NCO that others listen to and respect, someone who looks good on paper as well as in person. Get your own paperwork in order and make sure your packet is put together properly. Ask your UA (Unit Administrator) to help you with anything that you need. If you don't have a good UA, then you can always go to USAREC website and look for the paperwork you will need. This site has some videos and slide-shows that will help you through the process.

For the high school students, future soldiers, or curious civilians who want to be Army pilots, the slots are a little bit easier to come by, although you may need to be willing to wait. When America is not at war, the Army normally doesn't have as many flight openings. Sometimes recruiters will have a long time before certain slots become available. Warrant officer applicants have the option to sign up for what we call "Street to Seat," which means that even if a Warrant Officer has little to no aviation experience, they can still get an aviation slot.

If you walk into a recruiting office, always be respectful, listen carefully to the information they have to give you, but never let them influence your decision. They are not the salesperson in the situation, you are. Their job is to fill the ranks. If your goal is to become an Army Aviator, make sure that the only contract you sign specifically states that you will be assigned a slot at Army Flight School. Even though a recruiter can't guarantee that you will be able to fly helicopters, they can promise you a flight school slot pending your success at Warrant Officer Candidate School.

If you aspire to be a commissioned Officer in the Army, then the difficulty of the challenges you will face depend on the component you choose to serve under. For those who don't know, Active Army, Army Reserves, and Army National Guard are three different components, all served by different recruiters. If you want to be an active duty officer, you can enlist as a cadet and work your way through Basic Training and OCS competing for the slot. Although you may be incredibly qualified and you easily beat out the competition, the challenge you may face is that sometimes there are no slots available for you class, which means even if you graduate number one of your class, there are no aviation slots for that time and your dreams of Rucker will be gone. If you go through ROTC, you compete over a longer period of time, against a much larger group of people, but there are obviously more slots available to the competitors. The OML (Order of Merit List) is a very complicated grading system, which will be fully explained during your years in ROTC.

Whether you get your commission from ROTC or OCS you must decide whether to join the active military, National Guard, or the Army Reserves. Army Reserves and National

Guard units only require that you get a slot in their unit before commissioning. In order to have a slot saved for you during ROTC, you will need to secure a vacancy hold. This is a form that will allow you to assess directly into the company you secure a hold with. After interviewing with their commander, you will complete more paperwork and get more information on the details necessary to secure your future. Once you become an Army officer, you will be sent to flight school. You might have to wait, you might go immediately, but you will get a spot. I went through ROTC while I was already in an aviation unit. I enlisted in the Army and was assigned to a unit in Clearwater as a Private. When I came back from Initial Entry Training, I joined ROTC. As soon as I commissioned, I went to Basic Officer Leaders Course, BOLC, and began waiting for my turn at Fort Rucker. The only competition involved is finding a unit.

Depending on your situation or your career aspirations, your route to Rucker is not an easy one. It's a road on which you will often encounter the answer "No." In the Army we like to say that "No" just means "Ask someone else." Follow your dream, be respectful and consistent; then do your best to succeed.

Getting a Home

Once you know you're on your way, you'll probably be preparing and wondering what the next step is for a young (or not so young) soldier on the road to being the next Nightstalker. Some people who are inexperienced or just don't care, end up being taken advantage of by people who are looking to make a profit. Many people are good business people, really do genuinely want to help, and will give an American soldier a great deal on living expenses. This guide will give you the best options I've seen based on my experience.

When I went to Rucker, there were only six people showing up at the same time as me. I was the first person of the six to report, and I knew nobody else on the list, and only one person in Alabama. If you know anybody currently in flight school, I recommend asking them if you can stay on their couch for a week while you get to Rucker and explore your options. The Army does have a program that will allow you to take up to ten days, depending on your orders, to go find a place to live. They can reimburse you for living expenses like food and a hotel while you are searching. This can be a long drawn out process so I would only use this method if you're comfortable with the Defense Travel System, and have the money to burn in the meantime. That being said, there are some consistent truths that flight school students learn, regardless of when you go to school. For instance, living off post, or off the military installation, will be cheaper. Living on post will be closer.

When I went to Rucker, I lived on post. I was stuck in a situation where I didn't know anybody, didn't have the time to search, and took the convenient way. I stayed in a community on post where I shared a duplex with someone who didn't have access to my side of the house. I had two bedrooms all to myself. This privacy was very nice when I needed time to study or wanted to have my girlfriend up to visit for a long weekend. There will be times in flight school when this privacy is very useful and very nice to have. I also had the added security of gate guards around the base 24/7/365. Nobody was granted access through those gates without being seen on camera and without being vetted. However, I also expended every cent the military gave me for housing. For me this was almost one thousand dollars every month that went through my bank, that I was taxed on by the US government, but I never got to see.

You can also accept a roommate on post and share the rent. This allows you to keep half of your BAH or Basic Allowance for Housing. Living on post is also a lot closer to the airfield if you already know that you want to fly Black Hawks. Waiting in line to get on post at certain gates, certain times of the day can turn the five minute drive I made for the latter part of my schooling, into over an hour, depending on when you need to show up for class or where exactly you live in relation to the field. In my personal experience, the money I could have saved living off post wasn't worth the convenience of proximity. Although, the office I had to deal with was terrible! They were not very helpful where I was.

My experience with the property people must be taken with a grain of salt because they may or may not be the same when you get there, and each person has a different experience based on their needs, negotiations, and ability to communicate effectively. I never had to lock my doors, and I never had to worry about loud neighbors or parties happening through my streets.

Many of my friends lived off post. The most common place is a road called Freedom Drive, just outside the Enterprise Gate. You can do a small internet search for these places and see which ones are most recently renovated, most vacant or most appealing to your particular needs at the time of your arrival. I highly suggest contacting these housing units before you ship out and decide ahead of time where you want to live. They can even match you up with a flight school student who will arrive at the same time as you to make sure your rent is the cheapest, and you save the most money from your BAH.

My friends off post had consistently more room, and on average, saved around $200 a month more than I. To give you exact numbers, my friend on Freedom Drive paid $800 a month while I paid $960. He shared his apartment, so he saved $560 a month, which went directly into his pocket (BAH = $960). Rent will most likely change during the time that you are there on post, as you will be there for more than a year in almost every occasion. However, if you have a lease off post, you could probably negotiate a price that won't change until you move out. Living off post allows for more freedom under the watchful eye of big brother as well, if you're the type of soldier who likes to let loose on the weekends.

A third option is purchasing a living space and then selling it when you're ready to leave. In my experience, only a few officers take the option of purchasing a small home and living there for the year or so until they graduate. The few times I've encountered these people, they chose mobile homes. There are many places to park a mobile home and usually they can be purchased at a reasonable cost. If you take care of it and are already an experienced home buyer, this very well might be the best financial option. You can purchase a home, use your BAH to build the equity and sell it later for close to or even the same price you paid for it. This allows to you keep most of the BAH that you will be taxed on as regular income.

This does not allow much space for entertaining, so this choice is usually best for single soldiers who spend most of their social lives at friends' homes or out on the town; and spend most of their study time in the library. There will be long work days and sometimes long periods of inactivity spent at Fort Rucker, so this mobile home could end up being barely used, or it can become a prison of boredom. The officer who let me in on this clever little secret ended up selling his mobile home for more than he paid originally, which netted him around $25,000 more because of the equity and sales bonus. I, however, am not an experienced real estate guru, so I took what was easy instead of what was smart.

Those rates will almost definitely be different by the time you arrive at Rucker. However, many people say the same things after they've left. Some soldiers would never have chosen differently, some soldiers wish they'd known ahead of time so they could have made a better decision.

Family and roommates are another factor to consider when you choose your housing, so be very careful in your decision. Not everyone who lives off post is a student, but many people in that town are working because of the aviation community that Rucker has created. If you have a family, they will most likely become an integral part of your success or failure as an aviator. Some families become stronger at Rucker because they learn to work together to achieve the common goal, others are torn apart because either the soldier or the support system cannot cope with the stress and obstacles the US Army will present. The Army tries to make programs to help families, but in my very limited experience I've seen many relationships fall apart due to the military. You need to include an extra person or your family in your considerations because Fort Rucker can very rarely be conquered alone.

Most students study with one or more study buddies. Roommates will save you money, but will also be in your space when you may least expect or want them to be. Roommates can help you study, help you wake up on time, help keep your schedule in sync, and help you graduate. Money is not always the only consideration. Almost every family on post is that of flight school students or the instructors stationed there, many of whom are military or former-military. Not everyone in the community surrounding the base is a student or temporary guest.

You'll need to consider your own personal study habits and social expectations as well as your financial situation when you make the decision to live on or off post. If you live off post, there are some places I recommend in the buyer's guide in *Appendix A*.

If you decide to live on post, your choices will likely be limited by whether or not you have a family, whether or not you have a roommate, or the housing community representatives in building 5700 (the main hub for in and out processing on post).

Training Outside of Flight

Once you find a nice home and you finish in-processing, you will probably be wondering when you'll get to try hovering for the first time. Everyone wants to jump in those birds and auto rotate, but there is some red tape you need to cut through.

First of all let's discuss Army PT. If you're what we call a PT stud, then feel free to skip this paragraph because you already know enough about fitness. For those who don't score a 300 on their fitness test on a regular basis (a perfect Army physical fitness evaluation score) you can expect to lose 30 to 40 points at Fort Rucker. PT isn't something you do on a scheduled basis once flight training starts. You need a passing PT score before you get to flight school, another one as soon as you get to flight school, one right before aircraft selection, and one more before graduation. Self-discipline is essential and this is an easy way to earn yourself more points.

For those soldiers competing for their slots (active duty soldiers) you will be ranked on everything that is scored during flight school. Most people forget to count the points because they become more focused on passing than being the best. Your original PT score, Basic Officer Leaders Course (BOLC) test scores, academics throughout flight school, and flying check rides all count toward what you end up being selected for. If your scores are on the high end leading up to your advanced airframe, you will earn the first choice for selection, which I will cover later; and after that, your scores count towards your choice for duty stations.

It is important that you at least maintain a passing PT score, which many fail to do. While I was at Rucker, if a person failed a PT test, they were immediately put on hold, placed into a remedial PT program and made to take a PT test every month for the rest of flight school, regardless of how soon they passed the test. This means that if you get drunk the night before selection because you're in the reserves and already know where you're going, you can still be subjected to programmed physical training and monthly tests for the remaining six to twelve months until you leave. Fail twice and you can be sent home. All the work you've put in may end up having been for naught if you fail to make the choice to run and work out on your own for the first time in your life. It happens!

Aside from PT, you will have BOLC, Dunker, and SERE training to complete in addition to getting to go defy a little gravity. Basic Officer Leaders Course used to be combined into a big class. I myself had been to BOLC in Texas as a medical officer, because I am a medevac pilot. That means I was able to skip a large portion of this part of the course. I jumped ahead about five weeks of training, which is actually pretty inconsequential in the long run.

Today, BOLC is split between officers and warrant officers. This gives you a good two months to distinguish yourself from the surrounding competitors while the stress level is low, the classes are boring, and the tests are easy. If you wish to be the lead student and get your first choice of airframes during selection, I suggest studying during this portion as much as you possibly can to get very high scores. Many people feel that during this period they don't need to study to succeed, and many soldiers won't work their butts off for something they know they can complete without the extra effort.

In the Army we like to work smarter, not harder. If you are a hard-nosed son of a gun, then extend your lead while you have the opportunity, because when it comes to flying, some people get it and some people don't. You never know which one you're going to be, even if you have flight experience. Some of the worst flight school students were prior pilots, fixed wing and rotary. They tend to think they know the deal and don't take well to new instruction. BOLC used to take place before flight training, but they moved it to the end of flight training during the middle of my run at Rucker.

Things change all the time, so by the time you go, it may or may not still be in that order. However, the coursework hasn't changed very much in a long time. The end result will still be the same; you will learn to be a good officer. You will learn essential aviator skills and decision making processes necessary for an Army leader. This will most likely seem like the most boring part of training, but it is also a good time to study 5s and 9s (which I will cover later).

It has been rumored for a long time that Dunker training will no longer be a part of flight school, however, this has been the case for many years, and yet it is still part of the school.

Dunker school will teach you to survive if the aircraft goes down over the water. If you're not a good swimmer or you are afraid of the water, this may present a challenge for you. Dunker school rarely eliminates people from flight school, because peoples' drive to become a pilot will usually outweigh their panic in the pool. The instructors are willing to work with you during this day-long course as long as you're willing to put in the work with the instructors. This course isn't something that you need to worry about unless you're terrified of being underwater. In that case I suggest taking a swimming lessons or practicing with a qualified life guard prior to going to Rucker. If the course is still in the curriculum you will be expected to pass. You're not expected to be good at Dunker before you get there.

SERE training is a highly guarded secret. The more you read about SERE school, the less effective the training will be. The more people that write about SERE school, the less effective our soldiers will be. Many people are afraid of SERE before, during, and sometimes even after they complete the training. My best advice on this matter is to GFY (Go Find out Yourself). They will give you what you need to know in advance when you get to Fort Rucker. The experts who run the course are much more qualified to talk about it than anyone who has simply experienced the training.

With all that being said, most people have a small idea of what SERE is and what they can expect to experience there. In the interest of the country, our brothers and sisters overseas, and our national security, I implore you to refrain from divulging anything about the SERE course after you have completed it. Many soldiers break this rule to some extent, although nobody ever admits to doing so. Each person who reveals details about this course weakens the integrity of the school and the training it provides. Many people talk about it with their families when they get back, or friends that aren't in the military and think, "This person can't possibly affect anything related to national security." However, in today's climate and information buffet, it's best to just avoid the subject. Listen to what the instructors tell you when they give you the original SERE brief. I encourage you to ask as many questions as you want, regardless of how other students in the brief or even the instructors make you feel about it. It's your training, it's your future, take it seriously.

MDMP stands for Military Decision Making Process. Whether BOLC is before or after (right now it's both) you go fly, this is a huge exercise that you will have to complete before you are eligible to graduate and get your wings. This exercise can be an easy walk through, or the bane of your existence depending upon how you approach it. Most military soldiers have gone through some type of MDMP process before. When I completed the Rucker version, I happened to be in a group with exceptionally laid back cadre. (Cadre are just the instructors in a particular military course or environment.) This allowed many of my group to avoid a large portion of the work and nonsense. If the cadre assigned to your group is more stringent, your experience may turn out to be more frustrating. Some of the cadre instruct the course as though their two weeks of instruction are going to change your life. A secret for you, they won't. Nobody I've ever spoken to has ever said, "Yeah, those two weeks at flight school were the best part of my aviation development and totally shaped my career." Don't misunderstand me, it is absolutely valuable training, but in my opinion it is structured in a manner that wastes lots of your time. A good way to avoid this waste of time would be to volunteer to be the leader of your group. Make the decisions and split up the responsibilities yourself so that you suffer due to someone else's inefficiency at doing so, because chances are, you won't agree with everything they choose to do. One way many people got around the unnecessary waste of time during the course was by scheduling doctors' appointments, out-processing meetings, and other obligations that couldn't be negotiated, missing much of the day with a legitimate excuse. We simply assigned their work ahead of time, they completed it while they were in the room, and when their product was finished, they were allowed to leave. I myself went to a wedding and ended up missing the culminating event, where most of the stress of the course resides. I'm not suggesting skipping out on learning the content, you can and should learn it, but they don't tell you that you'll probably forget much of what you're learning because you won't use that level of MDMP until you're a colonel. So if you don't end up remaining in the Army until you become a colonel it is unlikely that you would ever need this exercise. Unfortunately, the information contained in this portion of your training won't help you prepare for what you will face during your first few months at your new unit.

In summary, aside from flying, the training that you have to undergo is just as important as the flying itself, because the grades and test scores you receive count towards your ranking against your classmates. You should take every training section seriously as you face it and do your best regardless of how important you feel the training is and whether or not you will retain it afterwards. Sometimes you learn something in a course and forget it for years until one day down the line it saves your life. Never take anything you learn at Rucker for granted.

Instructors, Pilots, and Cadre

Once you've completed SERE school, kept your cool through Dunker, passed a few tests, and suffered through some boredom, you will get to meet your Instructor Pilot (IP). For TH-67s and BWS, the Army uses a company called URS to train their pilots. These guys are almost all retired Army pilots with more hours than they can generally remember. They have military trainers for each and every military aircraft. That means that all of your instructors were once warrant officers or commissioned officers whose job it was to fly the airframe you're learning in. Most of these instructors have been flying for three to five years and are at Rucker as a stepping stone in their career.

With the URS guys, you tend to have an older crowd. This means that they went through flight school a very long time ago and tend to have had a rougher time. The Army used to be a lot harder before everyone was concerned with how much stress it caused and how many feelings got hurt in the process.

URS instructors expect more from you, and usually don't care how much stress they cause in the cockpit. Just communicate if their style of teaching doesn't work for you. They all like their cushy job, with its six-hour work day, two-week off period, and generally awesome atmosphere. If they can't produce good pilots, they're not much use to the company they work for; so secretly, every single one of them wants you to succeed as much if not more than you do. They're invested in you.

These guys usually don't like students who aren't fully prepared. Although you may be thinking, "It's rotary winged aviation, who wouldn't be fully prepared?" I'm telling you right now that there is a whole library of information on aviation, and unless you have eidetic (photographic) memory, you will not have it all memorized before flight school. Later in the book I will present my suggestions on what to memorize beforehand. Getting an answer wrong that you didn't study the night before can set your whole day off and cause your flight to be much more stressful, like you're playing catch up, and result in making the training less productive.

People say that it is not how you fall that matters, but only that you get back up. This is very true with the old style IPs.

If you have a bad oral in the morning, be sure to shake it off and make the most out of your flight so that your training is worth your time. Do not let stress keep you back in your education or you may have a very difficult time finishing with a good score. You will develop a blind faith in your instructor with URS, especially in the beginning when you don't have flying experience. After a few near misses you will realize how good they truly are and why they are able to operate under higher stress conditions. Trusting that they know what's best is the easiest way to cope with the stress they may or may not cause you.

Do what they say regardless of how trivial it may seem, unless of course it is unlawful or unsafe. I have never heard of an instructor asking a student to do anything illegal or immoral, so this shouldn't be a problem, but blind faith should never be without common sense.

The military instructors are mostly younger pilots. Many of whom just finished flight school in the new millennium. This means they had smart phones and iPads to help them study, they are accustomed to the "new Army" or the "soft Army" as it has been called. (I happen to like this Army because I'm a laid back type of guy and a light atmosphere works better for my learning style.) My instructor through the Mike model course was much more like a friend than a boss. A UH-60M (Mike model) is just the newest version, the upgraded heli with auto-pilot.

Just don't forget that they are indeed, your boss and your future depends upon them. Never take advantage of their kindness. Show up on time, be respectful and study just as if you were getting yelled at for every incorrect answer. Military instructors also tend to structure the course in an Army fashion. Your brief in the morning will probably be more serious and later the instructors will be less intense.

These guys also train soldiers with the mission in mind. In the beginning, with URS instructors, you will be focused on aviation thought processes and preparation. You will be expected to study and learn everything you can about aircraft and how they operate. You won't really be correlating the knowledge into mission appropriate tasks just yet. When your instructors are military guys, they will be asking you why certain things happen and what purposes we have for certain procedures.

ASK QUESTIONS! The Army instructors have less experience, usually, than the guys from URS. You will find that they have to look things up, just like you do. They don't have the whole book memorized yet because they've probably been flying less than a decade. Military instructors love to fly. They love their work; if you can make their job easy, they will make your instruction fun.

A huge issue in Rucker is communication and coordination with Cadre. The people in charge of the flight line are not the people in charge of academics. The people in charge of academics are not the people in charge of students on hold, that is to say D Company (for officers) or B Company (for warrants), and none of them seem to know how to communicate with one another.

During the time before you fly and even once you start flying, coordination with academics and the flight line will be largely up to the class leader. I was the class leader all throughout primary and instrument phases, so for four months, I was the one making phone calls, making sure students were awake to make the 4:45 bus in the morning, and generally trying to be responsible for things that didn't affect me directly.

If you aren't the class leader, be sure that yours is a good leader. Have him communicate with the flight line and the academics and the hold cadre to make sure that your schedules aren't conflicting, that each individual leader knows where your class is supposed to be and when you guys are supposed to be there. For B Company, this always seemed to be a struggle. Although your class will most likely have warrant officers and officers all thrown in together, they will answer to different companies. B Co always seemed to have worse duties while students were on hold (in between courses) and never seemed to be able to organize their needs in a manner that was conducive to the best completion and usefulness for the students. D Co has its good cadre and bad cadre but on the whole, they are much more organized and hands off than the B Co, in my experience.

Surviving Primary

Certain things in the very first stage of flying are classified. Foreign students even have to use a different curriculum in their coursework due to the classified material. I'm not saying this to make myself sound important, but you must understand that this guide is not study material, and it isn't here to supplement any material you will need to pass the course; it is simply meant to prepare you and make you aware of what you can expect at flight school.

Primary, for me, and for many students, was a very stressful part of flight training. For many of us, it is the first time in an aircraft. It was the first time I had to really study as an adult. I graduated from USF with a bachelor's degree in Psychology and I still hadn't experienced studying the way you must if you want to become an Army aviator. That being said, remember that everything the Army puts out is at an eighth grade reading level, even if it does require a much higher level of understanding to comprehend. I've watched some real Neanderthals graduate flight school. Sometimes it surprises me how many people they really will trust with a multi-million dollar airframe.

The best thing you can do to prepare for Primary (the first section of real flight training) is work on your study habits and coping skills. This sounds elementary, but everyone learns differently. You need to figure out what kind of student you are, and use your strengths to pass the first part of your flight assessment. I'm an auditory learner, for instance. Meaning that reading something over and over takes me a lot longer to memorize than studying aloud with a partner. Maybe you learn better if you write things down or create a song. Whatever the case is for you, it will be beneficial to know going into the course so you don't have to figure it out during the course and get your ass chewed along the way.

The biggest thing people have trouble learning is not usually the principles of flying. You'll have that spoon fed to you in an academics course before you ever get to the flight line. Not everyone picks that stuff up immediately, but most people get the gist by the time it's necessary to be tested. If you are a person who requires extra studying for aerodynamic principles, aeromedical effects on the body, and flight rules and restrictions, I recommend the learning center on post. If your instructor deems it necessary, he can require you to go to the learning center for a recorded amount of time, and have you sign in and out on a log that will ensure you have showed up for study time. Avoid this mandated time wasting by doing the work yourself. When your IP asks you something, it's always best to be prepared. Some people have a hard time admitting they don't know something, don't make this mistake. As aviators, we're all type-A personality people. This means we like to succeed, we're usually competitive, and we don't like being wrong or looking foolish. Usually, this tends to make people give their best answer, even if they are unsure. In flight school, this can be good, or it can be a mistake, depending on your IP. Most pilots want you to know, not be pretty sure. Therefore, when you guess, you are digging a hole, or going down the rabbit hole as we call it. Many students try to explain what they do know and end up muddling it up or getting something else on the table so the instructor will ask about that instead. Do yourself a favor and fess up when you don't know. Some IPs are very laid back, which it makes for a great experience. All IPs expect your underlined steps to be learned and memorized, even if you don't understand what you're learning. This rote memorization without understanding usually is the toughest part for most students. I am not good at memorizing things I don't understand. It's like learning lines to a play in a language that you don't speak. It can be much easier when you know what it is you're saying. We pilots call these 5s and 9s. It is also known as limitations and emergency procedures. All the instructors are adamant on stressing that these two chapters of the book are non-negotiable. That sounds insurmountable right? How could one be expected to memorize two full chapters of a book. It can be done with a little help.

I recommend a study guide. I highly suggest two places at which most people end up spending (and in some cases wasting) a ton of money: Wings and the Hangar. Both shops have multiple locations in the Fort Rucker Area. It is important to understand that the documents these people sell are not military documents. They are supplements made directly from military documents. That means that the Army doesn't regulate what's in them. If you purchase an outdated study guide and learn the wrong thing, you will fail parts of your test, and they will not reimburse you or even care how you were affected. However, these stores wouldn't make very much money if they were selling products that didn't help everyone succeed. The guys who made these shops are Army pilots. A few of them are (or at least were when I was there) flight instructors themselves. I used the Hangar but many guys like Wings as well. The stores are pretty identical and put out much of the same information, but cover it differently. The shelves in these stores are covered in material and are a pretty big waste of money if you buy it all. The Army provides you with material so if you're going to waste time reading everything you get your hands on, just read your military pubs.

In primary, the book to have is Mr C's P2 check ride study guide flash cards. When I was there it had a blue cover with an orange and white TH-67 (bell 206 helicopter) on the front. If you're going to be in the Lakota transition (the military is slowly switching the aircraft they use for primary, due to all of our advanced airframes having dual engines) then this book isn't the only one you'll need. You should also pick up a 5s and 9s flash card set for each airframe you are going to fly. I would wait until you are sure you are going to fly a certain airframe before you waste money buying material, because these shops don't give refunds or returns. Mr C's contains the answers to almost every question you will be asked on the check ride that is required for you to pass Primary. I studied this book exclusively and I passed with over a 90%. Just so you know, almost nobody ever scores over a 95% or below a 75%, and the lowest passing grade is 70%. Every class usually has one or two guys who will need to take these check rides more than once but all the information is in Mr C's flashcards. Even after you move on to your advanced airframe, these cards contain information pertinent to every pilot, such as aeromed, federal rules, airspace, and other topics applicable outside of just the TH-67. Be sure to ask the girls behind the counter which flash cards are current; they usually walk you right to the one that everyone buys. If you get these cards ahead of time, however, you can be prepared going into primary, and can have a much more stress free time. Memorizing the underlined steps in chapter 9 and why they are important is crucial; it can save your own life in the event of an emergency, and it will help you pass the check ride with flying colors. Memorizing the limits in chapter 5 will help you know your airframe and make sure that you fly smart as well as help you correlate the information you're learning during the rest of the course. The helicopter will do whatever you tell it to (and sometimes things you don't tell it to) so if you fly beyond your limits or the limits of the aircraft you can very well kill yourself and everyone else on board just because you didn't know where that line was.

Daily questions are an annoying part of primary that will actually teach you a lot of good information. If your instructor doesn't care, you are more than welcome to do all of these questions ahead of time and knock them out at the beginning. They won't originally be understood, but at least they'll be complete and you will save yourself 45 minutes of work each night. You can always go back and look over your old work the day before those questions are due to review what you need to know for the next morning. My instructor wouldn't let us fill out the paper ahead of time, however, all the questions are given to you ahead of time so you can still go do the work and get the answers, then simply write them in as you go. I recommend this because you can sit in the back yard in a beach chair with a beer and knock the whole packet out over one weekend. It is one less thing on your daily to-do list to remember. There are a few places out there where the answers to these questions can be found online. I don't recommend this for two reasons: One, the point of daily questions is to force you to look through the books, which leads to you learning more than you intended just by hunting through them for the answer. Two, if you're caught cheating, you will immediately be tossed from the class, probably flight school, and most likely the Army shortly after your return home. The military has no room for cheaters or liars. I know successful pilots who used this method and didn't get caught, but I wouldn't recommend it. They change the questions all the time, sometimes not noticeably, but old answers stick out to the

IPs and might be very obvious if you get two, three, or four incorrect answers that line up with the old questions. I'm not trying to scare you here, but my instructor really did memorize every book he would ever need to reference. These guys have been teaching kids to fly for longer than some of us have been alive. The books rarely change, so when they change the questions, they notice. Copying another student's work is also considered cheating. Some IPs will tell you that working with your stick buddy is allowed and, in fact, resourceful. The difference lies in the matter of who is doing all the work. If you're both working, you're both learning and both considered good students. If the smart one does all the work and the instructor finds out you are carrying your friend by handing him the answers, you are both eligible for immediate elimination. Don't put yourself in danger of ruining your career or your stick buddy's career to save yourself a few minutes of homework every night. The honor code will be briefed to you, like everything else in the course, but not exactly laid out in the best way to emphasize this point. Again, I suggest completing the work ahead of time and reviewing the answers later, as long as you do the work yourself and, most importantly, do what your instructor asks. Cooperate and graduate.

Inside the aircraft is a whole other monster. Flying is not something everyone was born to do, despite what they may think or have been told their entire lives. Some people are just not meant to lift off the ground and be another eye in the sky. However, those with any semblance of hand eye coordination can be taught to control an aircraft. The fastest learners are usually those who played the most video games when they were kids (no, I'm not kidding, farm boys were slower to pick it up.) Climbing into a heli for the first time will usually have your butterflies (or pterodactyls in my case) flapping at full speed in your stomach. Your instructor is probably going to be some guy, older than the dinosaurs, who built the bird you're entrusting with your life. He's not going to be happy that you suck at flying, regardless of your lack of experience. Every time you accidentally try to kill him, you will most likely feel instant annoyance exuding from him. Learning can be very stressful when many of your instincts are working against you in the cockpit. You will need to relearn things at times; patience and communication are the best tools you can use to succeed during this initial phase of learning to fly.

We like to say a student has found the hover button once you figure out how to keep the aircraft in one place without your instructor's help. Finding this button takes some people a matter of days and others a matter of weeks. Some people don't know how to hover until a day or two before their first check ride, which is a month into the course. Stress is a given, how you handle it is the key to success. You must keep calm and communicate with your instructor without making life worse on yourself or your stick buddy (each student is given a partner to learn with, making the ratio of student to instructor 2 to 1.) Yelling in the cockpit is not only counterproductive, but dangerous, no matter who is yelling. Avoid angry remarks until after the flight is complete.

Some guys have great IPs for the first part of flight school, and I pray that happens for you. I did not. The first guy teaching me was the worst instructor I've ever flown with. Remember, being a good pilot doesn't make you a good teacher. Never be afraid of asking for an IP change. An IP change isn't something that is guaranteed, but it is a choice they can't refuse you if the conditions warrant it. It's also not something you want to overuse. They will brief you on the procedures for an IP change before you start flying, but it also comes with a stigma that most people are afraid to venture towards. I was the class leader, therefore, if I asked for a change, I was not only dumping a bad instructor on another student who might love his instructor, but I was also giving the impression to the rest of the class that I was more important than they were. I chose the high road and suffered through the experience.

I was wrong. It was a stupid mistake and cost me a lot of stress. It is imperative that you understand that becoming a good pilot is the most important reason that you are at Fort Rucker. Do not let your pride or feelings get in the way of accomplishing your goal. I know plenty of kids that did successfully change IPs (after primary I learned that it isn't a big deal).

If you are not learning, or simply hate coming to work in the morning, you need to ask for an IP change. If you can't pass the course because you can't focus, or you don't agree, or maybe your personality plain doesn't match, then you need to ask for a switch. Ignore the possible stigma and ensure yourself a successful outcome. This is where communication and patience really will come in handy. If your instructor is not suited to your learning style and personality, talk to him about it. "Sir, I'd like to have a discussion about your teaching methods when we land." If you don't communicate first with your instructor, your flight commander (the instructor's boss as well as your top authority at the flight line) isn't going to listen to requests of a change. Patience is necessary because regardless of how idiotic your instructor may seem, if you are indeed learning, your flight commander doesn't really care how annoying the guy is to you. He's known him longer, he's got to work with him when you're gone, and they're probably friends. Cooperate and graduate. Just remember, it is life and death every time you spin the blades. Taking off is optional, landing is mandatory.

Your solo flight in Army Flight School isn't a traditional solo. Every helicopter in our fleet is a two pilot aircraft. So your solo flight will still be with your stick buddy in the seat next to you. This is after your first check ride and it's a rite of passage and huge confidence booster. You'll be adept at hovering and pretty good at traffic patterns and radio calls by this point in the course. Your instructor will go on a quick practice run, get out of the front, set your stick buddy up next to you, give you a thumbs-up and you'll be off to the races. Three quick laps later and it'll be his turn to not kill you. Primary is all about teaching the students not to kill themselves in a helicopter. If you can master basic controls, rules, and principles of flying, you will get through primary. Despite my obvious dislike for my instructor, he provided us with a very nice certificate of our first solo flight with a picture of the aircraft we flew that day. It is a very proud moment in many aviators' careers and a fond memory that I will never forget. If you can survive your solo, you can survive flight school. This is the pinnacle of helicopter control and the rest of school is designed to teach you how to be more than just a pilot—to actually become an aviator.

Primary can be very difficult, as it was for me, or it can be very easy, as it was for some of the guys I was sitting no more than ten feet from. These guys weren't smarter than me, (most of them anyway) but they were better prepared. If you aren't willing to study, or not very good at studying it may require many techniques, including asking other instructors for help (which I recommend if you've tried everything else and you still aren't getting it.) Primary is usually where you learn what type of student you are and how you will approach the rest of flight school. Do yourself a favor, learn that ahead of time and do that part of the work when you don't have to worry about all the work primary will entail.

Surviving Instruments

Instrument flight, for those that don't yet know, is like driving a car from your house to a restaurant you've never been to, while staring only at the dashboard of your car. You use navigational radios and flight "instruments" to determine where you are in the sky. For some people, this was the hardest part of flight school, and really doesn't make any sense. For me, it was kind of easy; once you figure out the academic side of the coin, it will be easy for you too. Instrument academics is a splash back into boredom and a bit of a nuisance because you have no idea what they are talking about (usually). Patience and communication are important here because you need to continue to study and persevere in your attempt to gain understanding or you will struggle throughout the entire two months of this course. The first five weeks are in simulators and the last three weeks are in the air. That means you're not actually off the ground for over a month. Believe me, it goes quickly.

For me, being a fast learner who was generally good at math and quick to remember something once I've got a grasp on the concept, this was easy. For my stick buddy, it was annoying how good I made it seem. This guy told me during instruments that he wished he hadn't come to Rucker and that he'd rather go back home and be a cop instead. He said he regretted getting back into the military because the course was that annoying. He later went on to enjoy becoming a Black Hawk pilot and eventually graduated like the rest of us, but the stress does have very real consequences, so learn to manage it before you make any decisions.

The first evaluation you take is inside a simulator designed to teach you the skills necessary for controlling the aircraft for instrument flight. You get a week and half to master the fine control touch it takes to barely move the aircraft. For those of you in the TH-67 course, you will get used to using trim (a system that holds the flight controls in place for you) the correct way. The Lakota course may have students trimming the aircraft properly the entire time, but many of us in the Bell helicopters weren't used to letting the joystick fly for us until we got to instrument flight. All you need to do is practice not over controlling the helicopter, which you will probably do because Visual Flight Rules (VFR) flying is very loose and instrument flying is not. After you pass that check ride you'll have the remaining six and half weeks to learn things like lost communications procedures (what you do when your radios take the day off) and how to navigate if you can't see the tip of your blade disc. The general idea is that beacons and radio signals from machines that are in fixed points on the ground talk to receivers in your aircraft and by triangulating the direction, and sometimes exact distance, you can know where you are on a given map. For us, we were also taught to use the GPS. Civilian flight instructors don't always allow you to use the GPS because being able to read a moving screen of where you are doesn't ensure that you can cross tune VORs (a directional radio signal). By the end of the eight weeks of instrument flying you will become very familiar with these radios, instruments, and procedures.

The soldiers that did have trouble with this portion of the course utilized one another, their instructors, and the learning center, or library, to the maximum extent possible in order to pass. The crusty old farts behind the counter in the library usually have more flight time than most of your instructors. They only work there because they love flying, teaching, and are bored with sitting at home doing nothing. If you have trouble grasping the academic concepts, ask the academics instructors. Most of the instrument instructors will make private appointments to meet with students who are willing to learn more if you take the time to ask them. Your instructor is not always the most approachable person, and frankly not the easiest to request help from, due to your not wanting him to know how much you are struggling to retain. However, the instructor of the kid next to you will almost always be happy to help when you ask him, "Hey, Mr Soandso and I were talking about how to enter a holding pattern the other day, but I just didn't quite get it. Would you mind showing me how you decide which one to use?"

You will spend a great deal of time using the instrument study guides at Wings and the Hangar. Continue to study Mr C's flash cards because you're still flying and you're still responsible for everything you learned in the first two month course you took. Daily Questions in the instrument section are the same concept as the ones in primary, just different material. Handle them the same way. I never used a study guide from Wings or the Hangar because I studied alone and I understood the concepts behind the equipment and the procedures. The biggest thing I had trouble with was cockpit management and publications. I had to develop a shortcut sheet that I used on my kneeboard (a notepad that straps to the leg of every pilot) in order to maintain focus. You should develop your own method, feel free to use mine. I wrote it down on a card every day based on which frequencies were required to communicate with people wherever I went, and which radio frequencies would be required to navigate me to the next checkpoint. It looked like this:

Time Tune Turn Talk Torque (just a reminder)

	Nav 1	Nav 2	Com 1	Com 2
Location 1				
Location 2				
Location 3				

I needed to work pretty hard before I figured out the right way to fill out an instrument flight plan, even though the GP (Army pub for General Planning) tells you exactly how to do it. Always stick to the GP and your flight plan will never be incorrect. If you can back up your work in the GP, the IP will have to concede to your correctness. If he does it differently, he's breaking the law. Many check ride questions come from knowing where to find the information in the publications. That means that you don't actually need to know how long the airport runway is at every airport you fly to, but you do need to know where to look to find it. You don't have to memorize every procedure for lost commo, (most of them you will know because you will have discussed them so many times with your instructors anyway) but you do need to know where to find it. You will become exceptionally good at map reading during this course (something you can study ahead of time) and you'll even be able to navigate without seeing the ground by the time you're finished.

Instruments is complex, but doesn't have to be overly difficult. As soon as you have passed Primary and begun receiving instruction into instruments, familiarize yourself with the publications required (these you will learn are going to be the GP, the FIH or Flight Information Handbook, the IFR Supplement, and your IFR and VFR sectional charts) and the procedures necessary to pass instruments. Nothing can substitute for good hard work in this course, but if you stay ahead of the helicopter, as your instructors like to say, you will be fine and score very well on your check ride. I think I got a 91% when I passed instruments, but it was Thanksgiving weekend, it was late and I had a six hour drive ahead of me when I left that day, so I didn't really stick around to make sure.

Flight planning will be an annoying task the first few times you do it. Skyvector and Foreflight are two really good tools to shortcut some things that you will need to learn to do the hard way, the slow way, the way that no pilots ever use because it's less accurate and therefore less reliable. Foreflight costs money after you've wasted your free thirty day trial, and Skyvector usually has a disclaimer that says you can't use it for certain things. You, as a diligent student, will of course back yourself up with all the forms necessary for your class, but these tools can help you get heading, distances, times and calculations that you can do by yourself, but shouldn't have to. My eighth grade teacher used to say, "You won't always have a calculator everywhere you go." Smart phones weren't quite up and running yet. Your IP will probably say the same thing if you ask if it's cool to use your iPad as your kneeboard. "What if your electronics fail?" Well what if my map flies out the window? Same stuff different day. Always carry the paper copies and only use the electronics to save yourself time. Know how to use the paper. Computers are more accurate than your pencil and E6B (circular slide rule they issue that you're expected to become very familiar with).

The cockpit, like I said, gets busy. Don't worry about being stressed by this, most people initially are. My instructor had an amazing method for teaching instruments. He did most of the work and the cockpit management in the beginning, announcing everything he was doing and why. "I'm switching this radio to this frequency because we need information of the airport we're flying towards ahead of time." This helped me understand, memorize, and catch up when I wasn't sure what to do. The more we flew, the better we got and less he did. When he was confident we were ahead of the aircraft, which just means we were constantly preparing for the next step, he would sit back and let us fly the entire day without comment, just making corrections if we messed up, or making sure we had clearance if we'd forgotten to communicate something. They will never let you kill them; despite how hard some students try to crash into a tower, the instructors want to live, so have faith in their experience and trust their judgement.

The important part of instruments, like any good flight, is really where you're going for lunch. No joke, some instructors only fly to certain airfields because they have the best deals. If you have a good IP, you'll frequent a few places solely because they have the best lunch. I would ask your instructor if you could fly to Jack Edwards as well, if they still allow you to do so, because Jack Edwards always gives you free stuff when you land and refuel. Some places will be too far away, but if your stick buddy is sick one day, you might be able to make it to Tallahassee if you plan his flight as a straight line, full speed ahead dart. Tallahassee has a great FBO and if you call ahead they will have lunch prepared for you ahead of time when you land. Just remember that Wednesday is steak day and Friday is rib day at Andalusia, which I'm sure you'll learn by the time you get to instruments. One Wednesday they served bacon wrapped filet mignon, all you can eat for two bucks! The IP that night was offered to take home leftovers since they were closing and were going to throw out the extras. He took home five. Not all IPs like to go to these places, because they do get busy. The fuel companies make so much money off the flights the military training birds use, they really don't care how much it costs to feed you. So the best food places always get the most business. Usually if you plan your flight ahead of time, your instructor won't say no, unless you just re-use an old flight plan. I would advise against that because he'll make you go somewhere where the lunch isn't great, somewhere you've never been, or somewhere you hate flying into, just to teach you to change up your flight plan every day.

Before you've finished instruments, and usually before you even get halfway through, you will be briefed and almost propositioned to get an official FAA license. I SUGGEST YOU LISTEN. This card that they are going to offer you would cost about $140,000 on the outside, because civilians don't really have cheap access to Sikorsy's Black Hawk. Even if you're flying the Apache, Chinook, or maybe even just the Lakota, you need to take this test. The place is called PHPA, Professional Helicopter Pilots Association, and they spoon feed you a study guide that will help you get your license. There is a military shortcut in the CFR, or Code of Federal Regulation that allows us to apply for this license because we've received the proper training. You will not regret the $150-200 you spend getting this card, trust me!

So just like Primary, at the end of Instruments you'll need to study your butt off. Hard work is something required from aviators, even the bad ones. This time you will more than likely need more patience with yourself, as the instructors are more relaxed and the content is more complex. You'll need to communicate your struggles and misunderstandings effectively and early, or you can expect to take the check ride a few times. Once you pass this check ride, you will likely have a small respite from academics and this is where I recommend starting on your maps early.

Basic Warfighting Skills and Maps

BWS is probably the most fun you will have in flight school. It is a short, three and half week course, designed to teach you the fun of flying. You're finally trusted with understanding what you see on the complicated dashboard, and you're expected to be able to control the helicopter instead of it controlling you. The instructors know that the helicopter you fly in won't be your final airframe (the Army retired the Kiowa Warrior). They know you don't really care about these 5s and 9s because this is the last three weeks that you will need them. They also know that the maps you're using aren't ever going to be used that way again. For some, that doesn't always mean they will grant you any slack in creating them.

Maps are the first thing you see when you walk into the flight line at shell and find your seats. They give them to you a couple weeks in advance and tell you not to worry about maps until after your instrument check ride, which is good advice. You will then be expected to create what we call a "horse blanket" and use it to avoid flying into anything when you're floating a couple of hundred feet (sometimes significantly less) above the tree tops. These things are the bane of BWS and the biggest waste of time still used at Rucker. You will one day be flying with a glass cockpit (or TV screens used instead of dials and digital instruments) and they will have moving maps. Even in BWS, your solo will be assisted with a piece of equipment you wear opposite your kneeboard to guarantee that you never get lost without an instructor. However, the instructors will tell you that you're not making them just because they had to in their time, but that it teaches you to read the maps. I disagree. I believe the only thing tracing colored lines over a light table for roughly 30 hours only teaches you where to cut corners. You will learn to read the horse blanket, and you'll learn to navigate very well using the terrain beneath you. But first, you'll spend a lot of time in the learning center.

Making BWS maps is best approached after watching a few YouTube videos. One of the owners of the study guide stores, called Velocity Squared, puts out a great video on how to fold them and the best tips straight from the horse's mouth. He instructed the kids who sat behind me in class. You'll find that aviation is a very small world. They will tell you what to do, but I'm here to tell you what not to do. A good buddy of mine produced "the worst map in the history of flight school" as the instructors readily reminded him, and had to recreate his entire blanket from scratch. That was a good waste of thirty hours. DO NOT use just a red marker for everything in the books. The maps at the library are colored a certain way for a reason. DO NOT use the pens that your lighter will erase to draw the original hazards on your map. DO NOT buy the map making starter pack that they sell at Wings and the Hangar. These things cost around twenty or thirty dollars, but if you just buy the materials at office depot, you'll spend maybe five. What you'll need is listed out entirely in the buyer's guide.

Make sure that you figure out exactly what you need to do; ask questions early on and make sure you're doing it right. Some advice you can take or ignore is to ask someone from a class ahead of yours which route most of his flights traverse. The reason for this is that when you make these maps you will have about 30 different sections to trace over. Some take as little as three minutes, some take three hours. I can tell you right now that the horse blanket you make will be wildly unused. Work precisely on the ones you're going to need, and you can be a bit sloppier on the maps you never traverse. If your IP makes you go back and add more, then by all means, do it, but I've never heard of anyone going back to the library more than once. When I made my towers, I started by writing in all the altitudes. Don't. They don't matter and your instructors know where the towers are anyway. They'll tell you about ones that aren't listed and have you add them as well. I also realized that the little hash marks on the red wires (what you'll spend most of your time tracing) are actually really unnecessary since only a few roads or other boundaries are marked in red. I even marked some of the red roads black and nobody ever challenged it. Certain IPs want to see these hash marks; if yours does, you will know as soon as you show it to him, and he will send you back. You have an hour or two of hash marking to do, but it saved you that much time by not doing it in the first place and you are no further behind. What I did, was mark the hashes on any intersection so when I looked down, I could see which red lines were wires and which red lines were roads or boundaries. Again, my IP didn't care, yours might, do what you feel is worth the time, or better yet, just ask him.

I also didn't tape down my maps. The light tables you trace over have plenty of tape and clips so that you can have the most accurate traced horse blanket on the planet. However, you'll notice that for whatever reason, the grid squares on the maps at the library and the grid squares on your maps are slightly different sizes. This is supremely annoying and makes no sense, but in the end it doesn't matter. The difference is about ten meters when you actually get out there, and you're going to notice a road if you're ten meters from it, trust me. I left my maps loose, and they were, consequently a little sloppier, but I didn't waste any time untaping, retaping, unclipping, reclipping and generally worrying about a level of precision that won't matter at all. You'll save more time on tracing maps than you will reading this entire book if you take the short cuts I did. Now granted, I didn't take those short cuts in the beginning of this process, but as I said, it was Thanksgiving, I was going home for the holiday, and I wasn't about to work all week when I'm being charged leave for family time. There were guys with cleaner maps than mine, there were guys with messier maps than mine. It didn't make a darn bit of difference.

BWS is very fast. I learned all the material because my instructor asked me the check ride questions every day until I learned them all. He never cared if I got them wrong, because he knew if he repeated them enough, I'd have them by the end of the course. This was the IP I'd been waiting for—laid-back and very redundant. We never wasted time, were very regularly the first people out the door, and always had fun flying. He once took the controls from me in a field to hover over a hill and show me the den of turtles he had seen. BWS was awesome. You fly a more stable heli than the one you learned in, although it's almost identical, the blades are bigger and therefore have more lift. Memorize everything you can and if you want a study guide from the Hangar or Wings, ask the girls behind the counter which is their best seller for BWS. I don't recommend getting multiple guides for any part of the course, because they mostly contain the same information, and you'll end up focusing on only one anyway. The material isn't that difficult when you compare it to Primary and Instruments, but you do have significantly less time to learn it. For that reason, if you do require an IP change in BWS, do not hesitate, because you won't have time to relearn the course if you wait a couple of weeks into it.

You will get introduced into the Army's flight planning software in BWS. You'll have a couple of days in a classroom to ensure that you understand how to use it. In the beginning, this usually means you'll spend five or six hours planning the next day's flight, and quickly narrow it down to about forty five minutes after three or four tries at it. Very few people plan satisfactory flights with all the details required in half an hour. It happens, but most IPs want more. This software is very frustrating and if you spend an extra hour or so with the academics instructor who teaches this course, you will save yourself several hours of figuring things out the hard way at home on your own. Before you take this course, I urge to you take your laptop to a place where you can run all the updates that it will allow you to. If you get the software working on your computer you may think that it will be satisfactory, but old software could cause you an enormous amount of loading time. Anything the Army issues out is purchased by Uncle Sam from the lowest bidder, so remember that your computer isn't going to be a MacBook Pro and you need to do everything you can to stay updated so that you're not waiting on it and wasting time when you could be studying or relaxing.

BWS is usually remembered as the most fun people have before selection, and it's also the last check ride you get before you are set in the OML (order of merit list) that determines who gets to erase the first aircraft off the whiteboard. Use it to make sure that you competitive folks stay ahead or get ahead and remember that your career is being determined every day you get evaluated. Oh and remember that you will fly to different places for lunch most of these days as well, so plan wisely.

Selection

After BWS it will be evident whether you took my advice to invest some time and effort into maintaining a high level of fitness. You might be surprised at how much weight the PT score carries in the algorithm that determines the Order of Merit List, OML. You must pass a selection PT test before they decide who are the best and worst pilots in your class. You can be a rock pounding chimpanzee and rank well above half your class if you're the fittest rock pounding chimp in the school. Very few students scored 300 when we took this PT test; and scoring well helps after everyone else has slacked off and taken a 30 or 40 point hit to their average score. Most people don't work out as much when they encounter the long days and heavy workloads of flight school. I hope you're not one of those people.

Selection for Army National Guardsmen and Reservists is a formality. 95 times out of 100 they are only going to confirm what you already knew to be your airframe. However, changes do happen, and if you actually want to change airframes, there are ways of doing it. It is all about who you know. The branch manager can make a lot of changes if they feel so inclined, so figure out who yours is and don't be afraid to send an email. The worst they can do is tell you to buzz off and maybe inform your cadre that you're annoying them with silly questions, which is not a big deal at this point.

Sometimes you will be given a fixed wing slot straight out of nowhere. Most guys who are slotted to fly cargo planes, know ahead of time because they belong to units that have planes in them. No big surprise there. If you want a fixed wing position, start sending emails before you get to Rucker. They aren't easy to come by if you already belong to someone.

If you are competing for a slot, your OML position gives you power in the "erasing line." What I mean by this is that all the available aircraft are written on a whiteboard. Everyone who graduated BWS at the same time is sat down in a room. My class had about fifty students in it. The available aircraft for active duty service members are covered up until it's time to choose. The highest OML scoring student gets first pick. They'll call his or her name and he or she goes up and erases one of the aircraft, thereby filling that slot, taking the availability off the board and sometimes, your dreams with it. Don't react badly and cry if you don't get what you were hoping for. You'll quickly make yourself the laughing stock of the class and lose the respect of all the aviators who will one day be your comrades, leaders, and sometimes the people asked to follow you into battle. You don't want to have to earn their respect when they knew how immature you've been since flight school. Believe me, the community is small, if you fly long enough, you will see these people again.

Some classes have a good spread of choices, that is to say, an even number of Apaches, Black Hawks and Chinooks. Some classes have only one option, in which case, it doesn't really matter how hard you worked, you'll fly what they have space for. My class had one Chinook. It went second or third because it was like the golden goose. Less availability meant you must be cooler if you fly it. Some classes are all Apaches and some are all Black Hawks. I can tell you that the Army owns more Black Hawks than any other airframe. They are the most versatile, therefore the most useful, which is why we have so many. If you want to be an Apache Pilot, you have to outperform your classmates because there are usually fewer of them. Unusually, there was a class that was nothing but Apaches just a few weeks after us. Sometimes it's just the luck of the draw. The best thing you can do to prepare for this is to work as hard as you can so that if the choice is available, you can be the first one to make it. But don't worry, no matter what you fly, you will enjoy what you do, because flying for the Army is one of the best jobs you could ever have on this beautiful planet.

Advanced Airframe

After you figure out which steed you'll charge into battle with, you'll be given instruction on which publications to pick up and what to start studying. By this point in flight school you will know how important 5s and 9s are, so you will probably start there. Day 1 in the Hawk course is a 9 page test on chapters 5 and 9; you'll probably be spending a good deal of time figuring them out. The AKO (Army Knowledge Online, accessible only by CAC or secure password, created originally with a CAC) pages that the classes create are full of useful study material and tons of papers you must print before day one of classes. Because I am a Black Hawk pilot, I cannot speak specifically for the other classes. The Black Hawk course is usually known as the "easiest" course. Apaches have guns, so the course is twice as long. Part one learn to fly it, part two learn to shoot it. Chinooks are twice as big, therefore have twice as many systems, therefore more learning is definitely involved. The resources for those courses are just as plentiful, and you find them all in the same places, so this guide isn't exclusively for Black Hawk pilots.

When I went to the Hangar and told the lady behind the counter I was starting the Hawk course, I asked her to show me the flash cards that most people buy. You can probably tell by now that I like flash cards. You should also know that there are smart phone apps that have these flash cards in them as well as games to help you learn and memorize everything to do with your advanced airframe. I didn't purchase them because you never know what the person who created the app is doing in their spare time. Maybe they're updating the app with new information maybe not. You will absolutely have to update your flash cards when changes are published in your Army manuals, but at least you're in control of what is current and what isn't. I only bought one deck of flash cards, and I use them to study that material to this day at my regular unit; I've made mental notes of what's changed and what hasn't, but in the beginning it's best to have the most up to date material.

I got on AKO immediately and read what I needed to print before the first day. Certain things I recognized from my time in previous flight training, other things I didn't. Starting a Black Hawk takes a significantly longer time than starting a Bell

206, and if you can't start the bird, it's going to be really hard to get it off the ground. There will be videos on AKO. I suggest you watch them. There was a script for us. Download it and read it before you go to CPT (Cockpit Training). I never mentioned CPT earlier because it's not an essential preparation step that needs to be noted in Primary, however, you will receive it there as well. It's not very stressful, and very rarely found to be difficult. You will learn everything you need to know about it when you get there. Yes there is a week devoted just to starting the helicopter, just as there is Primary, but do not rely entirely on those instructors to teach you everything, because your first time it will take approximately 45 minutes, and you need to have certain things memorized when you sit down. 45 minutes is a lot of material to memorize so give yourself a good head start with the script and the video.

By the time day one of Contact (the Primary of advanced airframe) rolled around, I had my 5 and 9 test memorized and the start-up was foggy but I had a good base of knowledge. You will be going through systems academics around this point as well, so the work load only increases. You're expected to know everything you've learned up to this point (except aircraft specifics of the TH-67) plus new material on how the Army wants you to fly, not just how to keep the blades up and the wheels down. My contact IP was German. He was a bit of a tweaky guy who bounced a lot and smoked even more than he cursed. He had 3000 hours in Black Hawks and was smart as a whip. He also happened to be a bit of an annoying instructor because he an my new stick buddy liked to bicker and argue no matter how minuscule the issue. It was exhausting. However, he never let us put him in danger, we always survived, and we learned pretty effectively how to fly a Black Hawk.

The best tool you have at your disposal in this course is actually not one that you can purchase at Wings or the Hangar, but instead one that you get from the internet. The Army makes what they title the Flight Line Supplement and they give access to an updated version of the document to any soldier who has ever been through the course. This means I can log in to AKO years after I've graduated and download the newest material that tells me everything I need to know for the check ride. It has a breakdown of all the aircrafts systems, short study guides of chapters 5 and 9, as well as many aerodynamic principles and aeromedical information that is commonly accepted as "what is necessary" for pilots to know. It is pretty much a check ride cheat sheet that you can review to make sure you are in line when your turn to fly comes knocking.

Technically, the Aircrew Training Manual (ATM), tells you what you need to know for the check ride, but doesn't provide the material. Just the subject matter. The ATM is the military equivalent of the Practical Test Standards (PTS) that the FAA uses to judge civilian pilots. It will tell the reader the exact sequence of the examination, the subject matter the pilot is responsible for, and the standards to which the pilot must adhere in order to pass. None of the information is a secret to the students, but if you fail to read the ATM, you may not understand fully what is expected of you as you perform each individual task.

Contact allowed me to learn the ins and outs of what is expected of Army Aviators when we get to our units while also learning to control an aircraft that can lift up an armored HMMMV and fly it out of a valley. It will teach you the Army way of planning, preparing, and managing your flights. Each class gets to do a special exercise where you fly in formation before contact is complete. Our class received the Ranger Mission. You will have heard of this by the time you get to Contact because it happens every two or three classes. Flight school students plan, fly to, and transport a bunch of Ranger candidates during one of their training phases. You will learn about the different positions and responsibilities a pilot may hold while conducting a mission as well as learn to fly in formation and work with other pilots while in the air. In country, almost no helicopter ever flies alone anymore.

We got to fly down and pick up these starving Ranger candidates and feed them pizza and soda while they hopped in for a quick ten minute transport a few miles down the road. They were grateful, we felt like the coolest kids on earth and our instructors conducted the longest After Action Review (AAR) I've ever sat through. We also learned more in one day than any other day at Fort Rucker. I'm not exactly sure what happened to the candidates when they escaped our heli's and ran into the woods but a lot of IPs seemed to think they were smoked until they threw up all the pizza. Getting smoked in the Army just means getting worked until you're too tired to move. But I digress...

After Contact, you'll head into instruments for your advanced airframes, and after that you'll to do BCS. You guessed it, BCS is BWS and Instruments is Instruments. These courses aren't that much different from the first time around. Instruments is a bit shorter and BCS is shorter still. After these courses you go to nights. Surviving nights is all about seeing in the dark. The Nightstalkers, our special group of crazy aviators that take on the crazy missions you watch movies about, such as Black Hawk Down, are known for owning the darkness. You can't rightly go around flying blind, so you learn a whole new boat load of information about the human eye, changing light conditions and the devices the military uses to see at night. This part of the course is like learning to fly all over again because your references have changed and visual references are 80% of how your brain interprets where you are in space. Fortunately, for the first time since Primary, flying in the cockpit is harder than the material you will be expected to study outside the helicopter.

The most fun part of flight school, in my opinion, was nights, although it was also one of the worst parts of flight school for a few reasons. At night, you might as well have started flying all over again. Your references are different so your habits must now change. If you have a good instructor, he will have built in scanning techniques that are effective for night flying the entire time he was training you during the day. This way, when it comes time to turn off the lights, your scan is already set up and you don't have as much to catch up on. You are now learning to fly like an Army Aviator. When we're in country, we own the night. That is to say, if you can't fly at night, you can't be an Army pilot, because you will definitely have to fly in the dark.

During flight school, you will have learned almost everything you need to know at this point in your training. You'll be the most comfortable in the cockpit that you've been for last year or so, and you will be doing the same type of low level navigation as you were doing in BWS. If you're in a Black Hawk, this will get easy because Mike will be doing most of the work for you. (Mike is what we call our autopilot.) Just remember that you should always trust your instructor, but that doesn't mean he doesn't make mistakes. Many military accidents happen despite the vast amounts of experience in the cockpit. Guys get comfortable or skip steps and this can kill you. Night time is especially dangerous because it's harder to see and it's much easier to get disoriented. Communication is key.

Graduation

After advanced airframe you'll be expected to head off to your unit. A few weeks before your final check ride, sometime during nights, usually, but it does vary from class to class, you will receive your assignments. They'll tell you where you're going to spend the first years of your Army aviation career. Whether you'll be a platoon leader or a refrigerator king, you will definitely be expected to show up ready to learn. Just because you graduate doesn't mean you're ready to execute the mission. You will need to show up to your unit prepared for another 5 & 9 test, another PT test, and ready to progress through your particular unit's training regimen. Pinning your wings on will likely be one of the most memorable Army moments you experience. Only a handful of achievements in the military are more prestigious or take longer to obtain. Most people have their family pin their wings, so if at all possible, plan ahead and have someone you love and/or respect greatly show up to share the moment. It will be emotional even for the crustiest stoics in the class after everything you have put into becoming an aviator.

Remember back in the instrument phase when you spent your Saturday morning and took that test? Now's the time to cash in on their promise and go get your commercial rotary with instrument. Head over to building 5700 on post and get your flight records as soon as you step off the stage at graduation. Take them directly back to PHPA outside the Daleville gate and you will get all set up. You'll have an FAA certification in 45-60 days that allows you to get a job flying helicopters in the civilian world, if you're a reservist or nasty girl (which is what we call National Guardsmen).

Your final assessments may or may not ever reach the ears of your IPs at your first unit. They may or may not have any effect on how you are welcomed to that unit. You will be given several briefs, and loads of instruction on what to do once you leave Mother Rucker and head out to your new homes. I suggest following those instructions to the best of your ability. I mentioned self-discipline throughout this guide as one of the most important characteristics Army pilots must possess. Although, it should go without saying, I conclude by telling you that it is critical that you implement that specific trait at this junction in your career as an Army Pilot.

Getting Eliminated from the Program

Any good Non-Commissioned Officer that is planning on filing a Warrant Officer packet probably knows better than I do how to get into a little bit of trouble. Most soldiers have several stories of times when they were younger and almost threw away their entire career because of a dumb decision that they made while drinking, while out with friends, or while otherwise making an idiotic choice that they regretted later. Flight school is the very last place you ever want to mess up. By the time you have put in all the effort and work that it has taken to get to Fort Rucker, it would be a shame to lose it all on a five minute drive home when you had one drink with dinner at the Ruby Tuesdays in town. I can tell you now that the cops around this part of Alabama have nothing better to do than pull over flight school students. I know this because lots of them are nice guys, and will gladly have a conversation with you if you will take the time to talk to them. The crime rate in this community is very low. Most of the people who live there are aviation related people. Taking all that into account, it can be extremely easy for you to accidentally flush your future away by making the tiniest mistake.

Speeding on Fort Rucker can get your driving privileges on post revoked. A friend of mine had to ask his girlfriend to drive him to class for a few months because he was clocked at 35 in a 30. I used to set my cruise control at 30 MPH because it's really that regulated. It sounds paranoid, but the officers have a lot of time to dedicate to scrutinizing traffic; and it would be foolish to take that risk. Your leadership when you get there will reiterate to you constantly, "If we can't trust you in a car on the road, why should we trust you in the air with our soldiers?" Makes sense.

Drinking is a common activity for soldiers. We like beer. Who knew? However, any soldier that has ever been to the doctor's office on post knows that you are not allowed to say "recreationally" but instead are told to say "socially" when they ask how often you drink. If you are ever pulled over with alcohol in your system, it will be the end of your career, unless you know someone very high up who can pull a lot of strings. If you have an alcohol related incident while in flight school, you don't have to be caught driving, you can be kicked from flight school just for conduct unbecoming. It boils down to all aviators being excellent risk managers. If someone shows qualities that show they are at a higher risk for injury or accidents, then they are dangerous and won't be trusted with aircrafts.

Sexual Assault is a career killer in the military. Now most people would think, "I'm not that type of person, this will never be a problem for me." I would agree with you. You'll notice I didn't say that a conviction is a career killer. A simple accusation can end your Army career, even if you end up beating the case in the long run. The Army operates on Risk Management and if you have been accused of sexual assault, domestic violence, or even just getting into a bar fight on a Saturday night, you will most likely be terminated because you are a risky candidate. Flight School has no room for risks.

Also be aware that it can take months to defend yourself from this complicated type of UCMJ (Uniformed Code of Military Justice) suit. Exercise extreme caution. In my limited experience, I have known soldiers who have had to dedicate their entire career to fighting against a charge that would ultimately result in having their records ruined. For this reason, it is best to keep your personal social life separate from the Army, especially during your time at Fort Rucker.

Improper social media usage is a very easy way to get booted as well. This should go without saying, but never go to "questionable" websites on your Army laptop. They probably won't let you in, but if you were in high school during the early millennium, most of you know how to run a proxy. Trust me, they've thought of this and more, and you will get caught and probably reprimanded.

Aside from inappropriate use of military property, your own Facebook, Twitter, and even Snapchat accounts can and will get you sent home. I know a guy with an amazing beard that got pulled from training the very same day that the rest of us first stepped into a helicopter. He was on a funeral detail, a very honorable, but sometimes daunting task. This is basically when an old veteran passes on, as you've seen in the movies, the funeral is a very formal event. We like to send our brothers and sisters on properly, remembering everything they've done for us and their country. This particular soldier was annoyed at waking up so early and making the long drive, so he flipped off his cell phone and sent a snap to a girl he was seeing at the time that said "F*** Funerals" while he was in his Army Service Uniform or ASU. This girl (like many in the Enterprise area) happened to be the daughter of an esteemed Officer who just so happened to see the Snap. I'm sure he'd rather have a commercial Rotary wing license than a really cool beard.

"Cooperate and Graduate" is a popular flight school saying as well that I've mentioned a few times. IP changes are always available, and should be used, when necessary, but also with extreme caution. It would be wonderful to say the military was full of only exemplary leaders and that none of us ever had a character flaw or made a mistake. The reality is that everyone has character flaws and we make mistakes every day. The same goes for any officer, no matter how high up he may be. The story that follows will emphasize this point.

Jack's IP Change

Jack was pilot I knew, who requested an IP change in BWS. He was a very intelligent man, but he actually had trouble with rote memorization. His request was denied, so he continued through the course. He was not the easiest person to get along with. He had a knack for talking when he should not have; something pretty easy to do in a very stressful time, when you're working harder than you've ever worked in your life, and faced with more challenges at one time than you're used to dealing with.

Jack began to score poorly on his daily grade sheets so he requested an IP change a second time. He was denied. He continued to fly up until his check ride and was told he shouldn't take the check ride because he would fail it. He requested to be recycled so that he could receive training from a different IP and he was again, denied. When he tried to escalate the issue, to use the chain of command's open door policy, it only made the problem worse.

Jack did eventually pass BWS and later on the Hawk course, but he was almost ejected from flight school, despite his genuine yearning for education and success. If you are interpreted to be the slightest bit disrespectful or have the wrong attitude, it can ruin your career as easily as drinking on a Friday night.

He spoke to his officers back from his home unit asking for help and advice; and they spoke to the people at Rucker. Fortunately for Jack, the instructors at Rucker were more willing to listen to experienced officers.

There are two sides to every coin, so be very tactful when requesting help. If you're not able to cooperate with the rest of the aviators around you, you aren't going to be very much use to the Army, no matter smart you are.

How to Enjoy Your Time at Mother Rucker

They call it Mother Rucker because anyone who stays in aviation eventually returns to the nest. It is impossible to further your career without going back every once in a while to complete one course or another. The place can be your least favorite duty station or the most fun you've ever had, depending upon how you approach it. If you're a young single soldier, it will be easier to cope, but remember: You're there to fly, not make a child or find a spouse.

All joking aside, there are some really cool things to do in the Alabama area that you may not hear about until you're halfway through the course or even worse, almost finished. Most of you will be making a good amount of money, which you should invest wisely! But you shouldn't let great opportunities or experiences pass just to save some money. If you are the adventurous type, who likes to try new and different things, there is a great skydiving place about an hour south of Rucker that you should look up. Xtreme Skydiving is their tagline but if you run an internet search for Panama City Skydive, you will find them as well.

If you're not a rush junkie, or you're maybe just afraid of heights (you might not want to continue this career path), that's fine because Rucker still has a lot to do on post. The lake has a plentiful selection of boats you can rent at a great price. You can go waterskiing, wake boarding, tubing, cruising on a pontoon, or fishing from a kayak. All it takes is a short water safety exam, which they practically hand you the answers for. Lake Tholocco can be a great weekend activity for the summer or just a onetime event with your family.

There are also a good number of pools on post. Many of the ones in communities will require you to phone a friend, but you will almost definitely know someone who lives on post within a few minutes of arriving, so this shouldn't be an issue. There is also a great many places to hunt and fish on post if you're willing to take the time to get the licenses and permits required for each sport you're interested in.

For drinks, I recommend a place called Folklore Brewery. They're a great place out in Dothan that makes lots of their own brews and sells them to some of the local bars and stores you will probably visit at some point. They were close to finishing an expansion the last time I was there; and it was a great place to unwind and have some fun. They had corn-hole games, outside grill and music, and a large buffet that accepted donations. They talked about putting up a brick and mortar restaurant, so I would expect it to be an amazing place to eat within the next few years as well.

If a few drinks doesn't satisfy your thirst for a good party, remember that you're only two hours north of Panama City Beach, one of the biggest spring break party beaches in the country. The beaches there have been posting new regulations due to some of the incidents that occur. This is a good way to end your career if you're stupid, so don't take the risk if you can't handle yourself in a manner expected of an Army Aviator. However, of all of my buddies that did make this drive, none were disappointed.

Feel free to buy a football ticket to a college game while you're in the state. You will find out that there are two kinds of people in Bama: Tigers and The Tide. One of the biggest rivalries in college football cannot simply be ignored because your team is in California. I definitely encourage a good college tailgate and exciting game if you get the chance to visit one of the cities on your weekend during football season.

Enterprise also has a drive-in movie theater. These are fun for anyone who used to go to one when they were younger. You get two movies for the price of less than one in a traditional theater. I spent tons of time there because I love a good movie and a good deal.

There are some really interesting zoos in the surrounding states if you're into exotic animals. I understand this may be a moral dilemma for some people, but some of these zoos are actually big cat rescues and places where abused animals get help. These places tend to have different deals so definitely do an internet search before you visit. My girlfriend went with me to the Montgomery Zoo and fed giraffes, which she went absolutely crazy over.

The best place for sushi in the two towns, in my opinion, is right outside the Daleville gate by the pizza place and the donut shop. It's called Tokyo Sushi. You can get great lunch deals, but be careful because you'll end up spending more money than you should by going out to get sushi three days a week.

If you're a Christian, like me, then you may love to visit the Calvary Chapel in Enterprise. They're the only church I've ever been to that is located in a coffee shop. The community and fellowship there are amazing, even if you're not a Christian. The group of students and instructors that gather in that place create an amazing support system for young students, young families, or any type of person who needs a friend, a church, or a great cup of coffee. They do an excellent Wednesday night bible group that is a potluck every week. They always announce the theme on Sunday and people bring all sorts of food for mooches like me to fill up on before discussing life, flight school, relationships, and God. Even if you're just looking for a free meal on Wednesday night, I'm sure Pastor Steven would love for you to walk in his door. He might love to kick me for sending in a bunch of hungry mouths he wasn't prepared for, but he'd also love to talk to you about your life and your relationship with God.

If you're looking for a good training gym, I used to go to the Crossfit FXT that is behind Anytime fitness in Enterprise. They own the Anytime and they love flight school students. They gave military clients a great price, and were super understanding of any accommodations the military training might require. Check them out for staying in shape and keeping up that PT score.

Remember that no amount of fun will ever outweigh the regret that comes after a bad decision that ends your career, so manage yourself accordingly. Although it is very important to manage your stress, sometimes falling off a boat and getting the wrong injury can be just as deadly to an aviation career as a DUI.

Most IPs will advise working like a dog from sun up until it's time to get a full eight hours of sleep. Meaning don't stay up late to study, because flying tired or taking a check ride on three hours of rest is dangerous as well as dumb. Take Saturday completely off. Don't talk about flying; don't think about touching a book. Unwind. Spend the day with your family, your friends, or just yourself. Go to church on Sunday, or do whatever it is that you do on Sunday mornings, but Sunday afternoon, brush up and prepare for Monday morning. Then start over.

Summary

The purpose of this guide is to provide some initial insight into the struggles of a flight school student. If it has in any way encouraged you to bend or break the rules that the Army or the flight instructors lay down, I assure you, that was not my intent. I highly suggest that you do not do anything to damage your reputation, your integrity, or the Army. I hope that you will, after reading this, have a better picture of what Army flight school is like, and have a more thorough understanding of some of the tools that will be useful in succeeding. At the very least, you know which questions to ask, and a few things that the instructors either don't or won't tell you. If you want to become an aviator, I wish you the best of luck, which you won't need, because your work ethic will far outweigh your talent.

Appendix A: Buyers Guide

Apartments and Housing

On-post housing will be ran by Corvias military living. The options I discussed above should be considered, but no matter which neighborhood you live in, you will be paying through Corvias. I wasn't happy with the end result of my stay with them, however, everyone's experiences are different.

Off post housing options – Off post housing options will be changing constantly. My best suggestions are living near or on Freedom Drive. For all the single soldiers, if it is at all possible, I would reach out to your mentor at your unit, your assigned contact, or reporting officer, and try to get a contact list. Go on Facebook and create a group of everyone on that list and try to find people who are shipping out with you. Reach out to other like-minded soldiers who want to save some money, and try to find some roommates to go house-hunting with. The best deals are constantly changing due to the constant flow of in-coming and out-going pilots. If you have a family, I'd call the housing office at Fort Rucker and ask for the best place to house a family off post. They have contacts in their office who can help you look for a good piece of real estate.

Laundry Options

There is a guy who sells and buys back washer and dryer combos for people in the Fort Rucker area. He repairs them and turns them over for a profit. I did this when I went and it was fairly inexpensive after you consider how much laundry I did and the sell back price. I won't attach his number but Craigslist searches will usually turn him up. The address he operates out of is 4098 Rucker Blvd., Enterprise AL 36330.

I always used the on-post dry cleaners for my dry cleaning. They are located behind the gas station, right next to clothing and sales and the barber shop. You could also do a quick internet search of some laundromats because there are several around the small post.

Mechanics

On post there is an auto shop where you can use their lifts, their tools, and even their mechanics to help you change your oil, brakes, tires, and anything else you might need. They didn't do any glass work when I was there, but they are a great resource if you don't want to pay someone else an unreasonable amount every time you need a few filters. This place is back by where Bravo Company is, behind the soccer fields at Andrews gym. They're right next to the drive-through car wash.

SERE School

None of this is a secret, you will get a packing list before you go to SERE. Certain things you aren't allowed to go with, and certain things you aren't allowed to go without.

Knife: You will be using one heavily and may damage it so if you want your knife to be in good condition, don't go purchase some expensive Gerber before you go.

Books: There is supposed to be an approved list of reading material when you go to SERE, but they never really gave a hoot what we would read in our off time, and there was no barracks inspection, so I suggest a paperback or two.

Cotton Balls and Vaseline: You'll want to combine these two ingredients to make a nice little fire starter. This is a suggestion on the packing list, and one of the only things marked as an extra that I recommend actually buying.

In my limited opinion, this is all you should consider spending money on. You will be provided everything else that you need, and not be allowed or have time for much else so don't waste your money.

Primary/Instruments Study Material

Checklist protector sheaths and covers - Dark blue covers and clear sheaths that your instructors may suggest you buy to protect your checklist. I suggest that you buy at least one, but not for your TH-67 checklist. That little TH-67 checklist will be useless after primary and instruments and you will not be able to re-use the sheaths because ink manages to stick to the plastic and come off the paper. Buy the sheaths later during your advanced airframe so that you can use for print-outs of all your favorite short cuts that aren't in your official check list.

Mr C's flash cards for TH-67s - You can get these at either the Hangar or Wings

Laminated PPC - this is convenient and save you from having to print new ones every day, but eventually it will deteriorate after you erase and re-write over it, so you may need 2. They're less than five bucks. I loved mine. Also, many of the numbers will stay very close so you shouldn't have to re-write much.

Helicopter Flying Handbook and Instrument Flying Handbook - DO NOT BUY THESE! You can download them for free on the internet so paper copies are a waste of time. There is a lot of good material in here that I suggest you read, either before or during primary and instruments.

Map Making

Markers: Black, Red (2x), Blue, Yellow, Purple, Green, Orange (Not sharpies, they bleed through)

Pens: Buy a few of the pens that erase with fire. Your instructors know which. They're expensive but they are worth it. They're called Frixion pens.

Rubber Cement: The packs they make for you have three, I think. I used one. Most people use two.

Cutters: Use the ones at the library, don't buy them. If you go and someone else is using them, come back later, (working ahead will benefit you, procrastinating may cause you to wait for space to work for hours)

Packing tape: the clear kind, it's thin and strong, and if you watch the videos, you'll know where to put it. This part isn't essential, but my maps started falling apart by the time BWS was finished, and if you're flying Black Hawks, you'll need them to last longer.

Protractor: DO NOT BUY THIS, you can sign one out from the library, they have a million.

Advanced Airframe

Most of your material will be accessible through AKO. I suggest using that. You don't have to print it all out if you have an iPad you can get most of the files you'll use on there. If you don't have an iPad you will probably want to print out the flight line supplement.

Study Cards - The ones in the bright orange covers are the most popular. Just make sure you get the updated book with the most recent change to your manual. Again, available at Wings and the Hangar.

Nights

I went to the Hangar and bought a finger light, which cost me almost $80. I don't recommend this because a buddy of mine bought a tiny keychain light, the type you press your finger onto in order to turn on, and he had the exact same thing I did. He paid about two bucks for the light and two bucks for the Velcro strip that he glued to it. Sure mine was nicer, but the effect was the same in the cockpit.

By the time you get to your unit, they will probably offer to put a lip light on your helmet for free. They may also have certain SOPs about which things you can and can't use, so this may end up being a wasted $80, but the choice is yours.

Appendix B: Resources

http://www.goarmy.com/ - Go Army (Lots of good information for people who want to become soldiers)

https://www.us.army.mil/ - Army Knowledge Online

www.usarec.army.mil/ - US Army Recruiting Center

https://www.aviationweather.gov/ - Weather Site

http://www.ursrucker.com/ - URS (Company the Army uses for Primary IPs)

http://www.corviasmilitarylivinghq.com/ - On Post Housing

http://thehangar.com/ - The Hangar aviation gear

http://www.wings-aviation.com/ - Wings aviation gear

http://usacac.army.mil/organizations/cace/wocc/courses/wocs - Warrant Officer Candidate School

www.goarmy.com/ROTC - ROTC Website

https://www.faa.gov/regulations_policies/faa_regulations/ - Federal Aviation Regs

http://www.autorotate.org/Home.aspx - PHPA (license people)

www.usaa.com/ - USAA Federal Savings Bank

www.navyfederal.org/ - Navy Federal Credit Union

http://Armypubs.Army.mil/ - Army Publications (CAC required sometimes)

http://www.apd.Army.mil/ - Army Publishing Directorate

Appendix C: Expected Schedules

Hold Status

It will feel like most of your time is spent on hold status, and for some of you, that will be true. This schedule is usually what your day will look like if you aren't currently assigned to a detail. Newer students usually will be on a detail, and each respective company will put out the schedule for that detail in the company area.

Activity	Time
Wake up	5:45
PT Formation/Sign in	6:00
PT	6:00 - 7:00
Breakfast/Hygiene Time	7:00 - 9:00
Company Sign In	9:00 - 9:15
B Co Only Second Sign In	15:00

In primary, you will usually switch between morning and afternoon shift on a weekly basis.

Primary Morning Shift

Activity	Time
Wake up	4:00
Bus Stop (Two Busses)	4:45/5:00
Flight Line Morning Brief	6:00
Table Talk with IP	7:00
Take Off Time (on avg.)	8:00
Down Time	11:00
Bus Home/Lunch Begins	12:00
Academics	13:00
Release	15:30 - 16:00

Primary Afternoon Shift

Activity	Time
Wake up	6:00
Academics	7:00

Activity	Time
Lunch	10:30
Bus Stop (Two Busses)	11:00 & 11:00
Flight Line Brief	12:00
Table Talk with IP	13:00
Take Off Time (avg)	14:00
Down Time	17:00
Release/Bus Back	17:00-18:00

Instruments

For the first five weeks of instruments you will be in the simulators. Your schedules will be almost identical to the ones above, except that you will not spend as much time at the sim complex, because you don't have any aircraft to deal with. This means no preflight, no post flight, no aircraft issue and all the paperwork that goes with it everyday.

Morning Shift

Activity	Time
Wake up	4:00
Bus Stop (One Bus)	5:00

Activity	Time
Flight Line Morning Brief	6:00
Table Talk with IP	7:00
Sim Time Start	8:00
Sim Time Complete	11:30
Bus Home/Lunch Begins	12:00
Academics	13:00
Release	15:30 - 16:00

Afternoon Shift

Activity	Time
Wake up	6:00
Academics	7:00
Lunch	10:30
Bus Stop (One Bus)	11:00
Flight Line Brief	12:00
Table Talk with IP	13:00
Sim Time Start	14:00
Sim Time Complete	17:30
Release/Bus Back	17:45

Instrument Flight Line

The only difference is an extra bus in the afternoon shift to take you home.

Morning Shift

Activity	Time
Wake up	4:00
Bus Stop (Two Busses)	4:45/5:00
Flight Line Morning Brief	6:00
Table Talk with IP	7:00
Take Off Time (on avg.)	8:00
Down Time	11:00
Bus Home/Lunch Begins	12:00
Academics	13:00
Release	15:30 - 16:00

Afternoon Shift

Activity	Time
Wake up	6:00
Academics	7:00
Lunch	10:30
Bus Stop (Two Busses)	11:00 & 11:00
Flight Line Brief	12:00
Table Talk with IP	13:00
Take Off Time (avg)	14:00
Down Time	17:00
Release/Bus Back	18:00 (sometimes later)

Basic Warfighting Skills

In the beginning, we had to bus, and about two weeks into this course, you usually get to drive to the airfield. This saves you lots of time.

Morning Shift

Activity	Time
Wake up	4:00
Bus Stop	5:00
Flight Line Morning Brief	6:00

Activity	Time
Table Talk with IP	7:00
Take Off Time (on avg.)	8:00
Down Time	11:00
Bus Home/Lunch Begins	12:00
Academics	13:00
Release	15:30 - 16:00

Afternoon Shift

Activity	Time
Wake up	6:00
Academics	7:00
Lunch	10:30
Bus Stop	11:00
Flight Line Brief	12:00
Table Talk with IP	13:00
Take Off Time (avg)	14:00
Down Time	17:00
Release/Bus Back	17:00-18:00

Advanced Airframe

Morning Shift

With Academics (First 2-3 weeks)

Activity	Time
Wake up	6:00
Academics	7:00
Lunch	10:30
Flight Line Brief	11:00
Table Talk with IP	11:30
Take Off Time (avg)	12:30
Down Time	16:30
Release	17:30

After Academics

Activity	Time
Wake up	8:00
Flight Line Morning Brief	11:00
Table Talk with IP	11:30

Activity	Time
Take Off Time (on avg.)	12:30
Down Time	16:30
Release	17:30

Night Shift

Some classes will get put on the night shift for the instrument portion of advanced airframes because there is simply too much traffic to fit everyone in the day shift.

With Academics (First 2-3 Weeks)

Activity	Time
Wake up	12:00
Academics	13:00
Lunch	16:30
Flight Line Brief	17:00
Table Talk with IP	17:30
Take Off Time (avg)	18:30
Down Time	21:30
Release	22:30

Nights

This portion of the course is not the same as night shift, but actually flying nights, where you will be flying in the dark, so during the summer months, the times are adjusted to reflect when the sun goes down and it's actually dark out.

Activity	Time
Wake up	12:00
Academics	13:00
Lunch	16:30
Flight Line Brief	17:00
Table Talk with IP	17:30
Take Off Time (avg)	18:30 - 21:00 (summer)
Down Time	21:30 - 00:00 (summer)
Release	22:00 - 01:00 (summer)

Made in the USA
San Bernardino, CA
24 February 2020